AUSTRALIAN RAINFOREST ANIMALS

Mason Crest Publishers
www.masoncrest.com
Philadelphia

Mason Crest Publishers
370 Reed Road
Broomall, PA 19008
(866) MCP-BOOK (toll free)

First printing

ISBN 1-59084-213-8

Library of Congress Cataloging-in-Publication Data on file at the Library of Congress

First published by Steve Parish Publishing Pty Ltd
PO Box 1058, Archerfield BC
Queensland 4108, Australia
© Copyright Steve Parish Publishing Pty Ltd

Photography by Steve Parish, with
pp. 6, 24, 40-41, 42: Ian Morris
pp. 8, 10-11, 20, 26, 31 (Regent Bowerbird), 32, 33, 37
   (Boyd's Forest Dragon), 38, 43 (White-Lipped Tree Frog,
   male frog), 46, 47, 48: Stanley Breeden
p. 15: Peter Marsack (Lochman Transparencies)
pp. 21, 30: Raoul Slater
p. 23: Belinda Wright
pp. 27, 28, 29 (Eastern Whipbird), 31 (Golden
   Bowerbird): M & I Morcombe

Printed in Jordan

Writing, editing, design, and production by Steve Parish Publishing Pty Ltd, Australia

CONTENTS

Use of Capital Letters for Animal Names in this book
An animal's official common name begins with a capital letter.
Otherwise the name begins with a lowercase letter.

RAiNFOREST

Rainforests grow where there is plenty of rain. Australia has different sorts of rainforests. Some grow in warm places; others grow in cool places. These damp green rainforests are home to fascinating animals and plants.

Once there was a lot of rainforest in Eastern Australia. However, most of it has been chopped down, and many rainforest animals have become rare. Some people are now trying to save the rainforests.

◀ In the rainforest.

Nandroya Falls, North Queensland ▲

KANGAROOS AND WALLABiES

▲ Lumholtz's Tree Kangaroo

Some kangaroos live in rainforests. Kangaroos belong to a group of mammals called marsupials. A baby marsupial is tiny. It grows inside its mother's pouch until it is big enough to survive outside.

Tree kangaroos are rare. They live in the branches of rainforest trees in parts of North Queensland and New Guinea. The soles of a tree kangaroo's feet are covered with bumps so they can grip on to branches.

Swamp Wallabies are found in both hot, wet tropical rainforests and cool rainforests.

Swamp Wallaby ▶

POSSUMS

Possums are marsupials, too, whose babies spend the first part of their lives in their mothers' pouches. They live in trees and most of them eat leaves and fruit at night.

Ringtail possums can use their strong, curling tail to hold on to branches. The Striped Possum, which eats insects, cannot use its tail to hold on to branches.

Brushtail possums have bushy tails. Mountain Brushtail Possums are found in cool rainforests. They feed mainly on leaves.

▲ Striped Possum

▲ Daintree River Ringtail Possum

▲ Northern Ringtail Possum

Mountain Brushtail Possum ▶

The cuscus is a close relative of the possums. In Australia, cuscuses are found only in the rainforests of Cape York in Queensland. A cuscus has two thumbs which allow it to grasp branches easily. Like the ringtail possums, it can hold on to branches with its tail. Cuscuses eat leaves, flowers and fruit.

▲ Spotted Cuscus

10

FLYING FOXES

Flying foxes are big bats, which are mammals. They fly using wings of thin skin joining their fingers and their legs.

Mobs of flying foxes spend the day upside down hanging by their feet from a branch. At night, they fly off to find rainforest flowers and fruit to eat. Often, they must travel a long way to find food. They then fly back to their homes in the trees by dawn.

◀ ▲ Spectacled Flying Fox

Grey-Headed Flying Fox ▲

PLATYPUS

The Platypus lives in rainforest creeks. It has a leathery bill, and its eyes and nostrils are set on top of its head and bill. Its thick, soft fur keeps out water. When a Platypus hunts for food underwater, it closes its eyes and ears. Its sensitive bill picks up the tiny electrical signals from the bodies of the animals it eats. It stores its food in its cheek pouches and surfaces to eat.

The female Platypus nests in a burrow dug into the bank of the creek. She lays two white eggs. When they hatch, she feeds the babies milk from patches on her belly.

▲ Platypus swimming.

Platypus on the bank of a creek. ▶

ECLECTUS PARROT

Eclectus Parrots are colorful birds that live in a small area of tropical rainforest in North Queensland.

Like all parrots, on each foot they have two toes that point forwards and two that point backwards. This enables them to hold on safely when they perch on the branches of trees. They often hold food in one foot while they eat it.

The coloring of male and female Eclectus Parrots is so different that they look like different types of parrots.

The Eclectus Parrot shown at left is preening its feathers with its beak. Preening keeps the feathers clean and tidy so the bird can fly well. Tidy feathers also help keep out the rain.

▲ Male Eclectus Parrot preening.

Female Eclectus Parrot ▶

KiNG PARROT

Like all parrots, Australian King Parrots have a curved bill. Its sharp point helps crack the shells of the seeds they eat. They also eat fruit. When they fly, King Parrots make a loud call.

A pair of Australian King Parrots finds a tree hollow to use as a nest. After the female lays white eggs, the parents take turns sitting on them to keep them warm until they hatch. The parents carry food to their chicks. They feed them until their feathers are grown and they can fly from the nest to feed themselves.

◀ ▲ Australian King Parrot

ROBINS

▲ Grey-Headed Robin

▲ Flame Robin   Eastern Yellow Robin ▶

Australia's robins are small, plump birds that often sing at dawn. Some sorts of robins live in the rainforest, where they catch insects to eat.

In the spring, a pair of robins will choose a safe place to build a nest. They make the nest from strips of bark, bits of plants, and cobwebs. Many robins also put small pieces of green lichen or bark on the outsides of their nests. While the female robin sits on the eggs, the male brings her food. When the chicks hatch, both parents feed them insects.

PIGEONS & DOVES

Fruit-eating pigeons, like the Topknot Pigeon, fly through the rainforest in flocks looking for food. Then they feed on fruit in the treetops. The Emerald Dove waddles around the forest edges, feeding on fruits that have fallen to the ground.

A pair of pigeons builds a flimsy nest of thin sticks in a tree. The female lays two white eggs. When a chick hatches, it is hungry. A parent feeds the chick a special food it makes called pigeon's milk. Later, the chick is fed on fruit.

▲ Emerald Dove

▲ Topknot Pigeon

OWLS

Owls hunt for small animals at night. They search for food in the rainforest and along its edges, where it joins more open forest.

Their flight feathers have soft, fluffy edges, so owls make no sound when they hunt. They can see in dim light and they have good hearing. Owls can find prey just by tracking the noise it makes.

Owls lay their white eggs in hollows in trees. Australia has two different sorts of owls. Hawk owls have a separate circle of feathers around each eye. Barn owls' eyes are set in a heart-shaped disc of feathers.

◀ Boobook Owl   Young Rufous Owl ▲

Masked Owl ▲

KINGFISHERS

Kingfishers have big heads and long, sharp beaks. The Azure Kingfisher lives near rainforest streams. It perches over the water and dives to catch yabbies, frogs, and fish. It nests in a burrow in the riverbank.

The Buff-Breasted Paradise Kingfisher digs its nest hole on thc ground into a low mound built by termites. Both parents care for the eggs, and the chicks when they hatch. They feed the chicks insects and snails.

◀ Buff-Breasted Paradise Kingfisher

Azure Kingfisher with yabby. ▲

BiRDS WiTH LOUD VOiCES

◀ Green Catbird   Lyrebird ▲

Eastern Whipbird feeding chicks. ▲

Birds make their calls for different reasons. Many birds sing loudly to warn other birds to stay away from their home areas. The whipbird does this with a call that sounds like a whip cracking. Sometimes, a bird calls to say it is looking for a mate. The male Lyrebird copies the songs of other birds, as well as singing his own song, when he calls for a female. The male catbird makes a call that sounds like a cat meowing. A bird may make loud alarm calls that warn other birds of danger, such as snakes.

BOWERBIRDS

A male bowerbird builds a bower of twigs on the forest floor. He collects treasures, such as berries, bones, and glass, and places them around the bower. When a female comes, he sings and dances for her and shows her his treasures. If she likes him, she mates with him. Then she flies away and builds a nest for her eggs. She looks after the eggs and chicks by herself.

Male Regent Bowerbird ▲

◄ Male Satin Bowerbird

Male Golden Bowerbird ▲

CASSOWARY

The Southern Cassowary is a big rainforest bird that cannot fly. Its neck is blue and has two dangling, red wattles. On its head is a bony crest called a casque. The hole behind a cassowary's eye is the opening to its ear.

After the female cassowary lays her eggs, she goes away, and the male sits on them. When the eggs hatch, he looks after the striped chicks alone. He protects them from enemies and shows them where to find food.

◄ Southern Cassowary

Male Southern Cassowary with a chick. ▲

PYTHONS

▲ Green Python

▲ Carpet Python   Diamond Python ▶

Pythons are snakes with strong, muscular bodies. When a python is hungry, it flicks out its forked tongue. In this way, it can taste the scent an animal has left behind. As it follows the smell, little pits on the python's face feel the heat given out by the animal's body.

A python does not have poison glands. To kill its prey, it grabs an animal with its mouth, then coils its body around it and squeezes. The animal cannot breathe and it suffocates. Then, the python opens its mouth very wide and swallows the dead animal whole.

DRAGONS

▲ Boyd's Forest Dragon

Dragons are lizards that have strong legs and can run fast. They have long tails, and some have crests of large scales on their necks and down their backs. All dragons eat small animals, such as insects.

Rainforest dragons can hide by changing their color so that their skin looks like bark and their crest looks like lichen or moss.

◀ ▲ Southern Forest Dragon

GECKOS

Geckos are lizards with soft skins and big eyes. They have no eyelids, so they use their tongues to lick their eyes and to keep them clean. Geckos eat insects and other small animals. Some geckos have pads on their fingers and toes that help them climb. The skin of the Leaf-Tailed Gecko looks like bark covered with lichen, so it hides from its enemies by staying very still on a branch.

▲ Ringtailed Gecko

Leaf-Tailed Gecko ▶

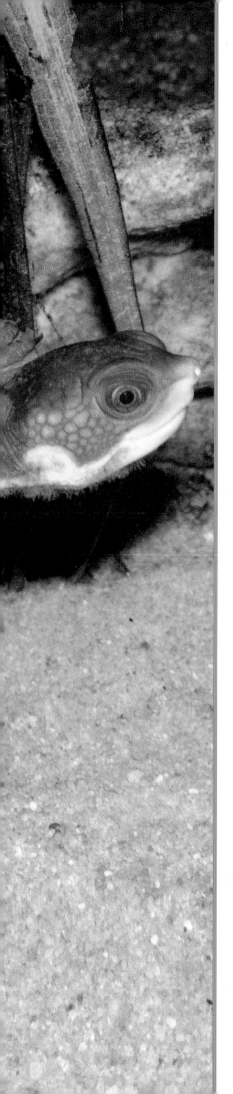

TURTLES

Rainforest rivers and streams are home to freshwater turtles. A turtle's body is hidden in its shell, which is called a carapace. Some turtles with short necks can pull their head between the edges of their shell. Turtles with long necks wrap their neck and head along the edge of their shell. This protects them from their enemies.

Turtles have webbed feet that help them swim. They eat animals, such as fish, frogs, and insects, that they catch in the water. Some turtles may eat fallen fruit. They leave the water to bask in the sun and to lay their eggs.

◀ A short-necked turtle   Eastern Long-Necked Turtle ▲

FROGS

Frogs have soft, moist skins and most of them live in damp places. When a male frog calls for a mate, he puffs out his throat. After frogs mate, their eggs hatch into tadpoles, which live in water. Tadpoles grow into adult frogs, which live in water and on land.

Many rainforest frogs have discs on their fingers and toes. These discs help them hold on to leaves and bark.

▲ Male frog calling.

▲ White-Lipped Tree Frog

◀ Red-Eyed Tree Frog

Dainty Green Tree Frog calling for a mate. ▲

FRESHWATER CRAYS

Crays are related to crabs and prawns. They belong to a group of animals called crustaceans. Crays have a hard outer skeleton on the outside. It protects them like a suit of armor.

They have 10 legs. The first pair of legs ends in big claws. Their eyes are on moveable stalks. They touch things with their long feelers to find out about them.

Freshwater crays lay eggs. The eggs hatch into tiny versions of the adults. This gives them a good chance to grow and survive if the water they live in dries up.

The colorful Lamington Plateau Cray may leave the stream it lives in and crawl over the forest floor. They have often been found far from any creek or river. If it feels it is in danger, the cray makes a loud, hissing noise and waves its claws to scare off the enemy.

Lamington Plateau Cray ▶

44

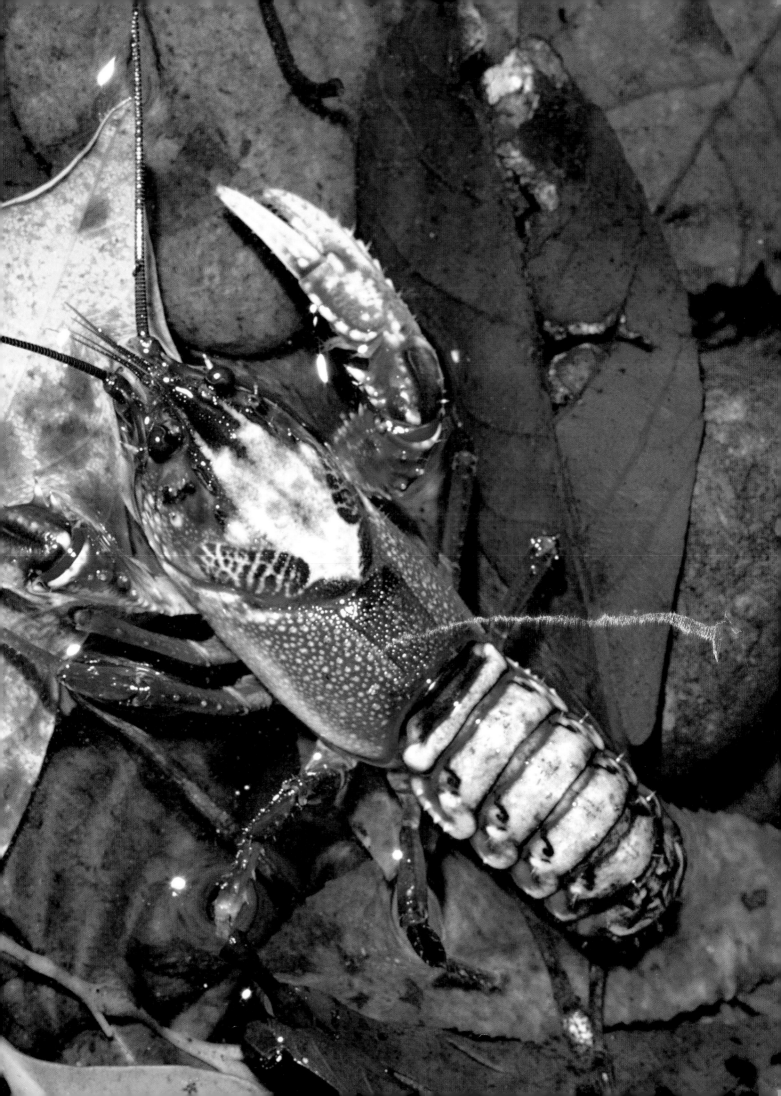

BUGS AND BEETLES

Bugs and beetles are insects. All insects have six legs. The body of an insect is divided into three parts: the head, thorax, and abdomen.

A bug has a beak, which it stabs into a plant or animal. Then it eats by sucking up the juices. A beetle has jaws and chews its food. Bugs hatch from their eggs as small versions of adult bugs. Beetles hatch as grubs, which grow and change into adult beetles.

◀ Jewel Bugs

Stag Beetle ▲

47

BUTTERFLIES

Butterflies are insects. Their long feelers end in little knobs. Butterflies eat the nectar from flowers.

After mating with a male, a female butterfly lays eggs. Each egg hatches into a caterpillar, which eats leaves. When it has grown, it changes into a pupa. The pupa rests inside a cocoon (or pupal case) as it changes into a butterfly. The case splits, and the butterfly comes out, dries its wings, and flies away.

▲ Union Jack Butterflies on pupal cases.

Cairns Birdwing Butterfly ▶

48

INDEX OF ANIMALS PICTURED

FURTHER READING & iNTERNET RESOURCES

For more information on Australia's animals, check out the following books and Web sites.

Arnold, Caroline. *Australian Animals*. (August 2000) HarperCollins Juvenile Books; ISBN: 0688167667

Seventeen unusual animals from Australia are introduced in this full-color book, including koalas, possums, gliders, quolls, Tasmanian devils, platypuses, echidnas, kangaroos, wombats, dingoes, snakes, and penguins.

Morpurgo, Michael, Christian Birmingham (illustrator). *Wombat Goes Walkabout*. (April 2000) Candlewick Press; ISBN: 0763611689

As Wombat wanders through the Australian bush in search of his mother, he encounters a variety of creatures demanding to know who he is and what he can do.

Langeland, Deidre, Frank Ordaz (illustrator), and Ranye Kaye (narrator). *Kangaroo Island: The Story of an Australian Mallee Forest*. (April 1998) Soundprints Corp. Audio; ISBN: 156899544X

As morning comes to Kangaroo Island following a thunderstorm, a mother kangaroo finds her lost baby, and a burned eucalyptus tree sprouts buds and becomes a new home for animals. The cassette that comes with the book adds sounds of sea lions barking, sea gulls calling, crickets humming, and even a raging forest fire.

Paul, Tessa. *Down Under (Animal Trackers Around the World)*. (May 1998) Crabtree Publishers; ISBN: 0865055963

The book features beautiful illustrations of each animal, its tracks, diet, and environment and includes interesting facts about how each animal lives. Australian animals featured include the platypus, the dingo, the kiwi, the kangaroo, the emu, the koala, the kookaburra, and the Tasmanian devil.

http://www.wildlife-australia.com/

This Web site is actually for the Chambers Wildlife Rainforest Lodge in Queensland, Australia, but it provides hundreds of links to all sorts of Australian rainforest creatures. From frogs to birds, reptiles to butterflies, if it lives in the Australian rainforests, you'll find in-depth information on it here.

http://rainforest-australia.com/

This other Web site for Chambers Wildlife Rainforest Lodge contains even more extensive information and photos on Australia's rainforest animals. Find information on the different levels of the rainforest environment; see pictures of the various creatures that inhabit each layer; and learn about Australian animals, from dingoes to lizards and everything in between.

http://www.masseycreek.com/fauna_2.asp

Massey Creek, a tropical upland rainforest property, is in one of Australia's World Heritage areas. This Web site has general information accompanying photos of some of the animals that live there.

http://www.rainforest.org.au/

The Australian Rainforest Conservation Society is dedicated to protecting, repairing, and restoring the rainforests of Australia. Viewers to this site can learn about Australia's rainforests and what steps have been taken so far by the Society to accomplish their mission.

http://www.austrop.org.au/daintree.htm

Daintree Forest—a small area of coastal lowland rainforest—has most of the endangered rainforest creatures in Australia and is under immense pressure to be cleared for private home sites. Viewers to this site can read about the controversy surrounding this beautiful land and find out what they can do to help in this campaign

NATURE KIDS SERIES

Birdlife

Australia is home to some of the most interesting, colorful, and noisy birds on earth. Discover some of the many different types, including parrots, kingfishers, and owls.

Frogs and Reptiles

Australia has a wide variety of environments, and there is at least one frog or reptile that calls each environment home. Discover the frogs and reptiles living in Australia.

Kangaroos and Wallabies

The kangaroo is one of the most well-known Australian creatures. Learn interesting facts about kangaroos and wallabies, a close cousin.

Marine Fish

The ocean surrounding Australia is home to all sorts of marine fish. Discover their interesting shapes, sizes, and colors, and learn about the different types of habitat in the ocean.

Rainforest Animals

Australia's rainforests are home to a wide range of animals, including snakes, birds, frogs, and wallabies. Discover a few of the creatures that call the rainforests home.

Rare & Endangered Wildlife

Animals all over the world need our help to keep from becoming extinct. Learn about the special creatures in Australia that are in danger of disappearing forever.

Sealife

Australia is surrounded by sea. As a result, there is an amazing variety of life that lives in these waters. Dolphins, crabs, reef fish, and eels are just a few of the animals highlighted in this book.

Wildlife

Australia is known for its unique creatures, such as the kangaroo and the koala. Read about these and other special creatures that call Australia home.